Are you my ne..

Life story
Written by Astrid Peerson

This autobiographical account wouldn't be possible without the help of my siblings, who took the time to share their memories of our lives with Douglas, and Barbara.

So I thank you for the information you gave me so I could complete this book.

I especially would like to thank my partner, who believed in me, and for telling me how proud he is that I have written my story.

Thank you to my foster parents, for always being there for me, and showing me how parents are truly meant to be. And for loving me as your own.

Although the title is 'Are you my new mum?', there is so much more to my story than my beginning, and my time in foster care.

I hope that my story as a whole can inspire people who are going through hard times, or have had a similar life to mine. Have faith that good can come from bad.

Him, her, and us.

I was born on Tuesday 18th September 1990, in King's College Hospital, London.

Born into an already large, struggling family, I was then the youngest of eight children, living in a mostly unfurnished multi-storey council house in Peckham, London.

Barbara and Douglas were far from the loving parents that every child deserves. Most parents love their children with every bone in their body.

They love with passion, and would absolutely do anything and everything for their child, or children.

Parents are supposed to keep their children safe.

Douglas, then ages 42, and Barbara just a few years younger, didn't even give us the bare minimum.

There was no love, no comfort, and no security,

Douglas would often spend the money he would receive from the government on alcohol, and cigarettes. Money that was supposed to be for bills, to buy the family food, clothes, nappies, or formula. It was rarely spent on us,

The cupboards in our house were often empty, and we had locks the fridge, that only her had access to. If anyone dared to attempt to get the food, they would be beaten.

My father had this awful, twisted sense of humour when it came to money. He would sometimes hide money around the house for his sick amusement.

The aim of his evil game?

Only IF you found the money, you could eat that day. If not, then went hungry... again.

My mother unfortunately did nothing to help the situation. She didn't even try to feed us when Douglas wasn't around. She had no money to even buy food for us.

Barbara never made any attempts to get us out.

He was in control.

I vaguely remember the house we lived in. There was one room, that was always dark, with a chair that only he could sit in. I tried to sit in this chair once, and he caught me. He picked me up, and put me on the floor. He had a strange dusty, and smoky smell to him, that I will never forget.

In another room, there was a mattress on the floor, placed directly in front of a large black-and-white television. One night I had just come from my brothers room, after eating an old sweet he had secretly stashed away, I was feeling really unwell, so I went to tell my parents. They were lying on the mattress, watching an old film.

I didn't tell them that my brother had any sweets, as I knew he'd be in for beating. So I just said I wasn't feeling to good. They allowed me to to lie with them, and placed in the middle of the mattress, but I had to face away from the TV. I was not allowed to watch it, at all.

I remember my mother telling me that the TV was just for adults, and that I had no business watching it.

There was a big, bright, and almost empty room. The windows had no curtains, no carpet was laid, but there was a pool table. A memory pops in to my head of my father playing a game of pool with one of his friends.

At the time, I was playing hide and seek. I hid behind a pile of rolled up carpets, waiting for my sister Claire who is closest in age to me, to find me.

I wasn't there for long, as I fell over and cut my cheek on some glass that was on the floor.

There was lots of blood, and lots of crying.

And strangely enough sympathy from my mother. She put me on the kitchen counter top, and grabbed a bottle of disinfectant from the otherwise bare cupboard, took the glass pieces from my cheek, and wiped my cut.

That is the only nice memory I have of Barbara. I'd say it was the only motherly thing she ever did for me. So there is that one nice memory of her being a mother, and then there is the mother who once left me in nursery.

Closing time came and went, but there I was, alone with the nursery teacher, crying my eyes out wondering why no-one was there to pick me up.

Had I been forgotten?

This nursery teacher wasn't the nicest of people either. She kept telling me to just stop crying, and made no attempts to comfort me, or distract me while we waited.

Eventually, my mother arrived, with one of my eldest sisters by her side. Both wearing smiles on their faces, acting as if they were on time, and everything was completely fine.

Barbara's excuse was simply that she had lost track of time. We were swiftly sent on way so that the nursery teacher could lock up, and leave. So, we made our way home. I didn't even get an apology. My mother didn't even care that I had been crying, and quite visibly upset.

Behind our house we had a garden, I don't remember using it much, if ever. But one day when walking through the kitchen, I saw through the garden door, a tent pitched up outside. Moments later, there I was, a very young child, sitting in this tent. I was amazed at how big it seemed. My brother was cooking sausages, and everyone was overly excited at even just the thought of having some food in the house, seeing as this was a rare, exciting, but also quite a scary occasion.

If Douglas had come home while this was happening, his shock would soon turn to rage, and the consequences would be dire, and someone would be beaten.

Douglas was a highly irascible beast, and would often turn his anger onto us, or Barbara. He had no time for us. Douglas was the sort of man who had the mindset that we shouldn't be seen, or heard. Well, unless he wanted our attention for his own benefit. He would often beat us, with whatever he felt like using at the time.

A belt, a slipper, a fist. A swift throw of baby on to a wall.

Barbara was merely a shell of a woman. She feared my father. He knew this, and enjoyed knowing that he had a lot of control over her.

He would often beat her as well, for many years, leaving her black and blue with bruises, only ever in places no-one could see. And she stayed with him. She continued to allow him to do as he pleased, to her, and to us.

Maybe she was scared, frightened of what might happen if she tried to escape. Maybe she wasn't sure if there was help out there for her, and us to safely get away.

I do know that she could have at least tried. She could have tried to get us out.

Instead, all of the Peerson siblings would try their best to protect each other from our nefarious father.

The older children tried so hard to take the beatings, so the younger children didn't have to go through it. But there were times, when Douglas would manage to get to us younger children as well.

The older children did the job that our mother should have done, but always failed to do. We were really close, and relied on each other. We only had each other.

I dread to think how life would have been if we hadn't had each other. What if there had only been one of us? How bad would the beatings have been then? How bad would the abuse have gotten if it wasn't shared between the many other siblings?

It doesn't even bear thinking about.

The streets

In 1993, we walked the streets of Peckham, innocently asking anyone who walked by for a bit of change.

Why didn't anyone question this?

No-one even thought to report what they were witnessing.

The streets were busy, cars whizzed by, people were rushing to get to their next destination, not paying attention to their surroundings. Completely ignoring anyone they passed. But there we all were, hand-in-hand, waling, and begging. Hoping to get enough money together to at least buy a bag of chips from a local fish and shop to share.

Have you ever seen children raiding the bins being supermarkets, eagerly searching for some edible food? We did this. We did this to survive, to fill our empty stomachs. Our Parents failed us in such a way, that this is what we had to do.

Claire, a year older than myself, only four years of age at the time, would try her best to feed me by any means, and would even sometimes steal food, just so I was fed.

Once, feeling incredibly brave, Claire made sure no-one was around before entering the pool room to steal some stale teddy- shaped biscuits for me to eat. Unfortunately, our father caught her feeding me, and she paid the price. But in Claire's eyes, it was worth it, because I was fed. Even if the food was stale.

Neighbours had their suspicions, about what went on in our house. They once gave Claire some money to get an ice cream from the van as it was doing it's rounds. Sadly, Douglas saw this happen.

He came charging out of the house, infuriated at what he had witnessed, grabbed my sister by her hair, and yanked her back into the house, into the pool room for her punishment.

Beaten, for attempting to get an ice cream.

There was a corner shop near where we lived. The lady who owned this shop always tried her best to give my sister food, but even she knew my sister couldn't be seen with too much food, so had to give a little amount each time.

For my sister, I was always her priority. Even though she was young herself, she would sometimes sneakily stealing orange juice, milk, and sometimes Cream Soda off the milk

truck, as the local milkman made his daily, early morning rounds.

When we weren't walking the streets of London, begging passers by for food, we would often spend our time walking the ground of The Imperial War Museum, taking any opportunity we had to beg the people inside for money, or for food.

We visited this museum many, many times. It was somewhere to go, and spend our days, so we weren't at home dealing with the abuse we often got from our father.

On the days that we went to school, we often arrived in a filthy state, and despite the school's many complaints about the way we looked, nothing ever changed. We still went in just as filthy as the day before.

The children would try to bully me for how I looked, Of course, they just saw an unwashed, dirty child wearing filthy clothes, while they were clean, and well kept. We were easy targets for bullying. I was an easier target for being so young.

Claire would be seen shouting, and beating on the children who bullied me, in the hopes of them learning their lesson, and never bothering me again.

I don't remember much about the school back then, But one other memoryI have is me walking the long hallways of the school, with a very annoyed teacher.

I scurried quickly behind her loud clickity-clackity shoes, looking at the classroom doors as we rushed by. Silently hoping that the next one would be the one we were heading to.

We were going to the classroom that Claire was in, to hand her back an item that she had let me borrow.

The teacher knocked on the door, impatiently waiting for the teacher inside to acknowledge her knocking.

Once the door was opened, I peeked inside, I saw Claire sitting on the carpeted floor with the rest of her class, looking slightly confused to see me standing there. The teacher explained why we were there, and ordered Claire to stand up so that she could get the item from me.

We were both told to keep our belongings to ourselves. Claire was then sent back to her place on the floor, and I was once again scurrying along behind the teacher, back to my classroom.

From that local Peckham school, they are the only memories I have.

Many children have the happy memories of going to parks with their families, having day trips, to really fun places, spending their days and evenings together laughing, and just enjoying the time they spent together.

In my memories, there are no fun days with loving parents. There were no park days, where all siblings happily run around together, playing games, chasing each other in the sun. Rolling around on the grass in fits of laughter, or even rolling down long steep hills, seeing who reaches the bottom first.

I am filled with the memories of walking the streets in all kinds of weather, wearing grubby clothes, no coat ever to be seen.

As an adult walking through those same streets I walked through as a young child, I often wonder what it must have looked like to see such young children in that state, asking for money, or food.

I have even made day trips with my children to the Imperial War Museum, where I would often go with my brothers and sisters to pass the time, before we had no choice but to go back to the house, where our father would possibly be waiting for us.

Every day we were locked out of that house, and away from our father, I still remember now how horrible it was, knowing that sooner or later, we would have to make our way back there. Never knowing what kind of mood he was going to be in. Never knowing what kind of horrible abuse was waiting for us.

Never knowing which one of us was going to be beaten , or abused, or both.

Slowly walking along the pavements, taking as long as we possibly could to get home, with these thoughts and questions in each of our heads.

Which brother or sister will we be trying to save this evening?

What state will he be in today?

Will he be drunk... still drinking?

Has he drunk too much, to the point of not being able to dish out the beatings he had planned?

Will his male friends be there? They enjoy the abuse too.

They were all just as dark, and ruthless as he was.

Twisted

The big, bright, almost empty room with no carpets laid, no curtains on the windows, and a pool table for Douglas and his friends to use.

This room wasn't just a room for my father, and his friends to play games of pool, or for on the odd occasion when he was in an okay mood, to let us in and play too. This large room was his 'go to' room, a place to carry out the abuse he inflicted on his children.

It became a room that us Peerson children feared. As we knew if we were taken in to this room, we would be beaten, or abused in the most unimaginable ways.

A child's innocence would continuously, and forcefully be taken away, by Douglas, and even some of his inhumane, friends, who were just as sick, evil, and morally bankrupt as he was.

As if the beatings on his children weren't enough for Douglas, he would also inflict inappropriate behaviour on to us. Some more than others.

Claire would try her very best to endure as much sexual abuse as possible, just so I didn't have to.

There was one night, where Claire unfortunately was not around to save me from the disgusting clutches of our father.

He got to me.

We were standing on the landing of our multi-storey council house. It was late in the evening, there was no-one else else around. Just him and I.

It was dark.

My father, the man I loved, the man who I wanted to love me, lured me towards him with a packet of chocolate sweets.

Now of course, being only three years of age, seeing chocolate sweets, I was so happy, and extremely excited. Not even just about the chocolate sweets he had, but also because he was being nice. He was offering me sweets.

Why was he offering me sweets?

I did not understand what was even happening to me. I was so young, a bright, blue-eyed, blonde, curly-haired little girl, standing in front of a man, wanting the sweets that he was offering.

That is the only time I remember being abused by father. I am unsure if that was in fact the only time, or if I have mentally blocked out any other abuse.

Even just being able to remember this one time, still sickens me to this day. It will forever be etched in to my memories, scarring me for life.

My siblings were also abused, they each had their share of despicable acts inflicted upon them.

Sometimes, or father would even invite his friends to join in on the abuse. They were always more than happy to join in, and carry out whatever sickening act they had planned with our father.

One evening, Claire was taken to the pool room. His friends were there, all eagerly waiting for her,

Slimy smiles were smeared across their faces. Each friend imagining the evil acts that they were about to perform on an innocent four year old child.

Claire was forcefully placed on to floor, lying down, looking up at our father, and his friends towering above her.

While one man forced Claire's mouth open, another man happily unzipped his trousers, and pissed into her mouth. Evil laughs filled the pool room, as each one of them enjoyed what the other was doing.

Claire was sexually abused that night. Her innocence take, in more ways than one.

Stolen, at the hands of adults who should have known better than to treat a child the way they did.

Never wanting to relive that moment in her life to anyone, Claire at the time, never knew that she would ever even have to.

More abuse would follow, from our father, and his friends. Day in, and day out.

Some times it was just him, and sometimes just his friends, with him watching.

Each man would regularly take their turn, over and over again, inflicting sickening acts upon their friend's children.

Not one of them ever had any remorse for what they were doing. Not one ever questioned it, or said to stop. Not one person ever reported it. They all kept it quiet, and kept it between themselves.

My father and hid friends were all extremely pleased with themselves during, snd after every attack.

They were all just as twisted as each other.

One night, I was taken into the room again, but this time, the abuse wasn't for me. The abuse was for David. I was forced to watch as my older brother was sexually assaulted by our father.

Forced to stand there, and watch, as his innocence was also taken.

1994

1993 came, and slowly went.

1994, now that any of us knew until it happened, was to be a very important year in our lives.

We were taken.

Taken from our parents, and placed together in a children's home. Were finally free from the beatings, and nasty abuse from our father.

We were taken once before, but it wasn't long before we were returned to our parents.

This time, it was for good. The happiest day of our lives so far, had finally arrived. After years of being abused, and neglected, someone had rescued us from that house, and that malevolent person who we called 'Dad'.

Social Services finally stepped up.

One day, there was a loud bang on our door.

Upon opening the door, we saw a few men, and women standing there, with the police waiting just behind them.

These people in front of the police officers were from Social Services. My parents had no choice but to let them all inside. Douglas was not happy about this.

When entering the house, most of these people had to cover their mouths, and noses, for they weren't used to the stench that filled the rooms.

I remember some of them coughing, and gagging from the smells that invaded their nostrils. Walking through the house, they all saw the state that each room was in. Filthy nappies were piled on the floors, Faeces were smeared across dirty walls. Flies buzzed loudly being wafted away by hands.

Social Services, couldn't believe what they had walked into. Despite many previous trips through the years to the house, this was the worst state they'd ever seen it in.

Our parents were arrested that day.

The police put the in handcuffs, shoved them into the back of police cars, and drove them to the local station.

We were all taken to a children's home in Sidcup, called Haven House. We had beds, actuals beds, not just a filthy mattress on the floor that didn't even have a sheet on.

The beds were nicely made, with duvets, pillows, and teddies neatly tucked up for us.

This place at the time was like a dream come true. We were fed, often. Three meals a day. We had baths regularly to keep clean. We were given clothes to wear, all the correct sizes, and not one item was dirty. Being here, at Haven House, our lives could finally begin, in a positive way.

We celebrated our birthdays, and we even got presents. One birthday came, and we were all equally full of such excitement.

We got ourselves ready in nice, smart clothes. I wore a dress. My lovely blonde hair, cut extremely short, due to Claire wanting to play hairdressers.

She used real scissors, and actually cut my hair off.

Claire was punished. But not by being beaten from our father this time. Someone who worked at the children's home said she had to have her hair cut short as well, to match mine.

She was upset, but it was a small punishment

compared to how our father would have reacted.

We spent the day at the party, rocking our short hair, faces covered in face paint that was slowly melting away, posing for pictures, and having the best day yet.

A party entertainer came. This person, was dressed as a clown. Claire hates clowns. She has a huge fear of them, for reasons unknown to me, they just scare her. She kept her distance all day.

This didn't ruin the day though. The rest of us thoroughly enjoyed the clowns entertainment. I was so happy, and amazed at the balloon animals, so much so that when the party was over, and it was time for bed, I took my balloon animal to my bedroom with me, and placed it on my bedside table, with a huge smile on my face.

The children's home was completely different to what we were used to. The workers there were all nice, and all very friendly.

Not that we knew until we left that is, but the workers created a memory folder for us. They filled the pages with many photographs of our time at the home, and the outings we had together. All complete with our own personal letter, detailing our time spent at the home, which workers we got on well with, and telling us about the things we most enjoyed whilst we were there.

The letter was finished with a list of names of all the people who worked at the children's home when I was there.

Unfortunately I later lost this memory folder due to the many moves I had, and at the time, not appreciating just how important it would be as an adult to look back on those memories, and share them with my children.

I now deeply regret not taking better care to keep the memory folder safe, and I so wish I could turn back time to get it back.

Apart

After a short 13 week stay at Haven House children's home, The Peerson siblings were separated.

Each one of us were sent to different areas of London. I went from the comfort of having my brothers and sisters around me all of the time, to being apart all of a sudden.

I was alone. I had no-one.

I was sent to an Irish lady in Bermondsey, London. I remember Aoife very well, she had lovely short, bright blonde hair, and a strong Irish accent. Aoife was very nice to me, which I appreciated. But this didn't not stop me from being shy. After everything I had been through, it took a lot for me to open up. She may have been my new foster carer, but she was still technically a stranger to me.

I stayed in a small room, with a bunk bed, I had the bottom bunk. Attached to the side of my bed, was a sticker chart, which I received a sticker for each night that I didn't wet my bed.

Aged 5, I was a bed wetter. Nearly every night, I would soak the sheets I slept on. I would wake up very wet, I obviously didn't want to constantly wet my bed, I just couldn't help it. I would often dream that I needed to use the toilet, but in my dream, I woke up, and made my way to the bathroom, and I did what needed to be done. Only to wake up and see that yes, it was a dream, and I had yet again, wet my bed.

The mornings that I woke up wet, I dreaded going to tell Aoife, just in case I would get in trouble. But, the mornings that I woke still dry as a bone, I would be over the moon. I would run to Aoife with a huge grin on my face, reaching ear to ear, telling her in the most excited way that I hadn't wet the bed. Off we would go, to my sticker chart, and place the sticker on that I chose. Only to wet the bed again the next night.

Aoife had another foster daughter who was already there when I arrived, she was a few years older than I was at the time, I don't remember ever speaking a single word to Hayley, and I don't have any memories of us even playing together. I just remember one evening sitting down at the table, eating party food. I can only imagine that it was her birthday.

At one point during my stay with Aoife's, one of my older brothers also came to stay.

David wasn't even with us for long.

On 21st October 1995, he left, and moved away to Kent. I don't remember the day that David arrived, and I don't even remember the day he left us. I only remember one day, with us getting ready for bed, and each waiting for our turn to have a bath. I was sat in the bathroom while David was washing himself, and he asked me to look at his private parts.

I laughed it off, and said no. I didn't want to look. David then proceeded to ask me if I wanted to put his penis into my mouth. I knew at this age that what he was asking me was wrong to do. So I went and told Aoife.

Maybe this was why he left so quickly.

Staying at Aoife's was never going to be for long. It was just a short term placement, while Social Services found me a more permanent home.

I don't think Aoife did anything with me while I stayed with her. We didn't really go on days out to any parks, days our shopping, we didn't sit together and watch films, or play games. I felt like even though Aoife was nice to me, she didn't really warm up to me, or care about me in the slightest.

Aoife told me that my mother had had another baby, and this baby would be coming to stay with us.

I was so excited, a baby, coming here, My new baby brother.

That excitement left as quickly as it came. I don't think Aoife managed very well with me, and a baby. Not long after he arrived, I was leaving.

I knew that Aoife's wasn't a long term placement, but at the time, I felt like I had just been replaced. Was I so bad that she could so easily be fed up with me just because a baby had arrived? Why couldn't she cope? I was a fairly easy child, despite everything I had gone through. I was a well-behaved child.

Apart from the frequent bed wetting, I was a good five year 5 old child. Well-behaved, well-mannered, and I was never naughty.

But Social Services were called, they were told that she simply could not cope with both of us. So I had to go. She did not want to look after a brother, and a sister at the same time.

To this day, my brother still lives with Aoife,

And I have not seen, or spoken to her in many, many years.

Another house

My bags are packed, ready to go to yet another house. Another family that were strangers to me. Another place for me to feel like I did not belong.

An outsider.

The Wood family. There was Toni, my foster mum. Danny, her son. And Gemma, her daughter.

I didn't see much of Danny, sometimes he was there, sometimes he wasn't. We didn't really speak much, if at all. I shared a room with Gemma, and just like Aoife's house, I had the bottom bunk.

Toni was quite short-tempered, I would often find myself being made to stand, or sit, and face the wall for something that she considered to be naughty. I don't remember ever actually being naughty at Toni's house though. I only ever remember her being very short-tempered with me.

It was like everything I did was an inconvenience to her.

Whereas her children, Danny, and Gemma, could do no wrong. They were both the perfect children in Toni's eyes.

Gemma would play football on Sundays with a local team for her age group. We would go every Sunday to watch her play, and I was so jealous because I thought that she was super cool playing football. I wanted to play in a team, just like her.

So I asked Toni if I could also join a local team for my age group. That was a very short conversation, as the answer I received was a firm no. I was given any explanation as to why I couldn't. The answer was no, and that was that. I asked a few more times, in the hopes of her changing her mind, but the answer never changed.

No, no, and no.

Despite desperately wanting to join a team, I gave up asking. Although, I never did understand why Gemma got to, and I couldn't. I was always treated so differently, it made me so upset. I did not like Toni at all.

One evening Danny, and Gemma got to have a chocolate from Toni's chocolate.i asked for one, but as always, I was met with the familiar answer of "no".

Off to bed I went, with tears in my eyes.

I thought to myself, "I've had enough."

I wanted chocolate. If Danny and Gemma got one, I wanted one too. I waited until the coast was clear, and made my way to Toni's chocolates. I sneakily grabbed one, shoved it in to my mouth, and gobbled away. I didn't even care that I would be caught. I only wanted one, so I took it. I made my way back to bed, and shortly after Gemma came, and got in to her bed.

With a smile on her face, Gemma asked me if I took a chocolate. I told the truth, and said I didn't care if Toni told me off, it wasn't fair that they got to have one, and I was left out.

A short while after that, Toni came in, asking questions about the missing chocolate. She Gemma if she knew who'd taken it, she shook her head, and stayed silent.

Toni then asked me, and I lied to her. I told her I didn't take the chocolate, I had been in bed, and hadn't left at all.She knew I was lying, and I was in big trouble. The next day I was made to sit, and face the wall all day. I was only allowed to leave to use the toilet, and had my breakfast, lunch, and dinner also facing the wall. If I dared to look at the TV, I was told to moved my head back to facing the wall.

I remember feeling so sad that this was how I was being treated. I always felt like I was treated far differently that Toni's actual children. They got everything, while I was mostly made to feel like I was in the way.

Like I was always such a nuisance, and Toni just didn't have the patience for me.

Not all days were bad at Toni's. She had a friend who would visit often with her two sons. Stephen, and Paul. I got on quite well with Stephen, as he was around the same age as me.

Every time they came to visit we'd spend as much time as we could playing in the garden. Stephen was my first crush, not that he knew, I never told him I liked him. At the time, we were just best friends. I never knew that the last time they visited, would be the last time that I would ever see them again, before I left for another home. We never even got to say goodbye.

I quite enjoyed school while I was living with Toni.

Fairlawn school in Forrest Hill, London.

I had the nicest friends, and at one point, I even had myself a little boyfriend. Well, we said we were boyfriend and girlfriend, really we were just really good friends.

Yep, five year old me, had a boyfriend. Tom was so nice to me. He always shared his water or juice with me on the days that I had none. I was always picked as his partner for class projects, and we'd always play together at break times.

I didn't know that I'd be leaving, and loving schools yet again. So I never got to say goodbye to the friends I had made at this school.

All these years later, I only remember their first names, so I've never been able to find them to get back in touch.

Although I wasn't in Fairlawn school for long, I have a few fond memories, some of me playing at break times, with the equipment we were given, singing songs with my friends, and my teacher. She was lovely, and always such a happy women. My teacher once bought in sugarcane for the class to look at, and one by one, we each had a little bit to taste. As well as a little lesson on where it came from.

We always had really fun lessons as well. She had ways to make learning a really good experience for the class.

On a weekday, I was told I was having the day off school, as my social worker would be coming to take me out for the morning.

We went to a little café, where we sat for a while, and spoke about how things were going at Toni's, and at school. After a short while we went back to Toni's, I went in to the kitchen to find all of my belongings in black bin bags.

This is why my social worker was here, this is why she had taken me out. So Toni had time to pack my things.

I cried. I begged. I wanted to stay. I told her I would be a good girl, if she let me stay, I would be so good, every single day.

I begged through so many tears.

Toni had absolutely no emotion. I was simply told that I had to go, I couldn't stay any longer. I later found out that she called Social Services, and told them she didn't want me anymore, and they had to find a new foster home for me as soon as possible.

Did she really not care for me at all? I was just a five year old child. Toni treated me so poorly. Despite me being a fairly good child, Toni just did not seem to like me.

To come home and find my belongings packed, was traumatising. I felt as though I was just being thrown away, without a single care in the world.

Toni did not seem to care how it would affect me. She didn't care that I was standing in front of her, crying and begging to stay. It seemed she simply just did not have any feelings whatsoever.

My belongings were all tightly packed into the social worker's small car, with me squished into the back seat.

And off we went.

The drive seem to take a long time. I spent the whole journey feeling sad about what had just happened to me. I wouldn't get to even see my friends again. I was at school one day, and gone the next.

We finally came to a stop. I was so nervous, once again having to start over.

Another house that wasn't my home.

Another hose without my siblings.

Another home I wouldn't belong to,

More strangers that weren't family.

We walked up to the big house, that had a big front garden full of colourful flowers. Through the side gate I saw a huge back garden that had a patio, and the patio went on to a big grass area. That was exciting to see.

The social worker rang the doorbell, and we stood there, waiting for the door to open.

Are you my new mum?

A lady answered the door with an excited look on her face. A smile that went from ear to ear.

She greeted us, and invited us in. The social worker quickly grabbed my belongings, dropped them off, and had to go. So I was left there alone with this lady.

She told me her name, Marjory. I asked her why she spoke in a funny way. Marjory explained to me that she came from a place up North, so she had an accent. I let out a slight smile, I thought her accent was funny.

"Are you hungry?" She asked me. "What's your favourite thing to eat?"

I told her that I really enjoyed spaghetti Bolognese. Marjory went over to the kitchen cupboard, pulled out a tin, and checked that it was the sort of spaghetti Bolognese that I liked .As she was opening the tin, I asked her the question that had been swirling around in my mind.

"Are you my new mum?" I asked her nervously, shaking inside at the thought of what her answer could be.

Marjory told me that she could be, if I wanted her to be. I was welcome to call her Mum, or Marjory, whatever I felt comfortable with.

After eating my food, I was shown around the house. There was the kitchen, a front room, a downstairs toilet that Marjory called a 'utility room', and upstairs had four bedrooms, and a bathroom. One of the bedrooms, Marjory said I was to share with her adopted daughter, Shelly. I hadn't met her yet, or Marjory's son Timmy, or her husband, Tim.

They were all at school, or work, so I had to wait for them to finish to be able to meet them.

Soon after I arrived, I we had to leave the house to pick up Marjory's grandchildren from the school up the road. They often came to hers after school whilst their parents, Marjory and Tim's oldest daughter and her husband, were working, and would pick them up later on in the evening.

Walking along the road, Marjory asked to hold my hand. That was a strange feeling. She said it was to keep me safe. I was so confused. An adult I barely knew actually cared about my safety?

We arrived at the school, and patiently waited outside of the school gates, for Marjory's grandchildren to come out.

One by one they walked up to see their nan standing there with me. They had no idea that she was going to be fostering another child. They were all very excited, and full of questions for me. I happily answered their questions, and we all quickly became friends.

Rachel was closest to me in age. I was only a year older, so we got on very well straight away. Rachel's older sister was called Becky, and then there was Eddie, their younger brother.

As the afternoon went on, Shelly, and Timmy came home from their schools, and they were introduced to me. We said our hellos, and off they went to their rooms.

Early in the evening Tim Marjory's husband, came home from work. Tim was a kind-looking man. He had his dark hair gelled back, Elvis-style, and a moustache covered the area between his nose, and mouth. I loved seeing the big grin that covered his face. It was always such a warm, lovely look.

I very quickly felt comfortable here. This house was different. It was a home. The people here were different. They were a family. I hadn't yet experienced this feeling, but it was one I was starting to like.

Marjory often tells me still, to this day, that she remembers seeing me for the first time, walking through the front door. A small, blue-eyed, blonde girl, nervously standing in front of her, and she just fell in love with me. She knew straight away that there was something special about me, and knew in her heart, that she wanted me to stay long term.

Me staying Marjory, and Tim's was never supposed to be a long term foster placement. Only ever a short term stay, while Social Services found me a forever home. I was extremely lucky to have found them, and that they very quickly grew to love me as though I was their own daughter.

The month was July, and schools were soon breaking up for the six weeks holidays. Marjory got me in to the local primary school that was just a few minutes walk up the road from where we lived.

I only had a week in year one before we broke up.

The first day of school for me was a good one. We had the loveliest teacher, he made me feel so welcome. Mr Phillips told Marjory that the stick on earrings I was wearing wouldn't be allowed, and unfortunately, I had to take them off. I didn't mind so much.

He showed me where to put my bag, and coat, and then showed me a spot on the carpet where I could sit, and wait for the other children to arrive.

I was the new kid. Everyone wanted to know who I was, and everyone had questions.

A girl sat down next to me, she already wanted to be my friend, and asked to play with me at break time. Obviously I said yes! It wasn't long though, before we drifted apart, and weren't as close as we were on the first day. But I did make more friends, who are still friends to this day.

Amber, and Sezer lived pretty close to me, but in opposite directions. I loved having friends who lived close by, so I was able to see them often.

And then there was Taylor. My first childhood love. Taylor was just an amazing person. He was so kind, and just so nice to everyone, especially me. We were fairly close throughout the years at Hurst Primary. We even got married in the school playground, but quickly divorced the same day.

Taylor was my on-and-off again primary school boyfriend, and honestly, he meant a lot to me, even as just a friend. We lost touch as we went on to secondary school, and didn't really talk much, if at all, ever again. But I'll always have the fond memories of us at school.

Sezer's dad owned a dry cleaning shop not far from where I lived. So I would often spend my days, or weekends with Sezer, at the shop, and playing outside. Her family were like my second family growing up. They always made me feel included, and loved. Sezer was the only girl, as she had two brothers. Ali was the eldest and Ersel was the youngest.

I grew up being just as close with them both as well.

As the years went on, I would often spend many weekends with Sezer, at her house in Lewisham, having sleepovers. And to this day, I am still in contact with sezer, her brothers, and even her mum, Sonay, who was like another mum to me. She will always hold a special place in my heart.

Amber, lived around the corner from me. I'd also spend time with her, at her house.

Amber had two sisters, Lauren, and Shelby, and two brothers, Sam, and Harrison. We'd all spend time in Ambers room, laughing, and messing around. Or in the garden, on her trampoline, pending hours jumping around.

Ambers parents were nice enough to to include me on a day out to Legoland once. And although I absolutely hate any fast, or high rides, I didn't really go on anything. I still had the best day, and loved that I had another good friend whose family would often include me, and also make me feel loved.

Although I often spent time with sezer, and amber, I also spent just as much time at Marjory and Tim's house. I would often be found in their large garden, or playing out the front of the house, with the children who lived in the houses down our street.

Cala Llonga

I'm still here, still living quite comfortably with
Marjory and Tim.

I seem to fit in very well here, at a good school, I
have good friends, and I'm being fostered by a
family who love me, and care for me.

This is home.

We are going on holiday. Two weeks in Cala
Llonga, Ibiza.a small island just off Spain, not the
party side to the island, the quiet side, where lots
of families go for a relaxing holiday.

I was so excited to be going on a a plane, but also
a little nervous. The flight wasn't a long one, just
over two house, and we had arrived. I remember
the feeling of the hot sun, and heat, smacking me
in the face as I left the aeroplane.

Soon after leaving the aeroplane, we had to go
and collect our suitcases, and then wait in the
taxi area, in a queue full of other families, all
waiting to get a taxi to their final destination.

Our final destination, was an apartment block in
Cala Llonga, called El Dango. Walking down the
small steep steps to our apartment, I was amazed
at the view in front of me. Everything looked
beautiful. We were so close to everything.

Nightly entertainment could be seen from our balcony, from the hotel opposite us, so I would sit there with some binoculars to see it a bit better.

The sea, and beach was just below us. The restaurants, and shops just a short walk away.

Every day there, we would wake up, eat breakfast, get ready, and go up to the pool area.

Even better, Marjory, and Tim's grandchildren, Becky, Rachel, and Eddie, were also there in their own apartment, with their parents, Deb is their mum, and Marjory and Tim's eldest Daughter, and Charles was her husband.

I spent every day playing in the pool with Rachel, and Eddie. Becky would spend her time with Shelly. Timmy had his own friends who he already knew from previous holidays in Cala Llonga.

As the evenings came, we would leave the pool, and get ready for dinner, were we often went to a restaurant to eat. The owners of the places we went to were all so friendly, and knew Marjory and Tim well. We would be greeted with huge smiles, and treated very well by everyone. I soon had a favourite restaurant. 'Up and In', with my two favourite waiters, Carlos, and Joe. Every year we went to Cala Llonga Carlos and Joe would be so happy to see me, and everyone else again.

wWe would visit the restaurant so much that they soon knew what I liked to eat.

"Would you like your usual?"

My answer was always a yes. My "usual" was pie, chips, gravy, and a Fanta lemon without ice.

I loved that they knew, and always remembered, despite knowing so many other people, and servings hundreds of people everyday.

Cala Llonga was a holiday we went on every year, for two weeks. Marjory and Tim had a time share on the apartment, so it just made sense. Other people also had timeshares, so also went every year around the same time as us. All the adults got on well, and so did all of the children, and we all looked forward to seeing each other again, year after year.

One year, our regular holiday was coming to an end, we all went out for dinner. Shelly was older now, so went for dinner with her friends to a different restaurant, and Timmy did the same.

This year Timmy brought his best friend along on the holiday. They were both out together at a different restaurant to us, where there were a few other teenagers looking to cause trouble. And they did just that.

A glass bottle was thrown towards Timmy's friend. Timmy jumped in the way, and the bottle smashed against his head. Marjory got the news of the situation, and Timmy was taken to the local hospital.

Everyone was leaving to go home. The holidays were over, but we of course, had to stay longer.

Timmy was okay, but the situation was a serious one.

The time share that Marjory and Tim had, was also rented out by other people throughout the year, and so we had to leave, and find another place to stay. Marjory frantically searched the other hotels nearby, hoping they had the room to spare for us to stay at such short notice.

We eventually found somewhere to stay. My favourite restaurant also had apartments that people for stay in, and luckily had room for us. So for the next two weeks, that was our home. If we weren't there, we were travelling to and from the hospital to visit Timmy every day.

Although I was happy that Timmy was okay, and he was getting better, I was so bored without any of my friends there. I had no-one my age to hang around with when we weren't at the hospital. I was so unbelievably bored!

Every night we would eat at the restaurant, they knew the situation, and all gave their best wishes. Carlos and Joe would often try and lift my spirits, and make me laugh. But I was still so bored without anyone there, it just wasn't the same. I wanted to go home. I couldn't wait to leave and get back to normal.

The time came after two extra weeks of staying at Cala Llonga, for us to go back home. I was so excited.

When we got home, everyone was so jealous of my tan, and they all had a million questions. All wondering what I got up to during the extra time I had there.

Unfortunately, there was no fun news to tell.

Hospital, apartment, dinner, bed, and repeat the next day.

The day after arriving home, I had school, and everyone again was jealous of my tan, wondering, and questioning me where I had been on holiday, and why I was there for so long.

I didn't tell anyone the reason, I just said that we decided to stay a little bit longer. I felt like no-one really needed to know to the actual reason. It wasn't anyone's business.

The questions soon stopped, and my tan slowly faded away.

Even as we went back to Calla Llonga the following year, everyone there, from the returning families, to the waiters, and waitresses, all asked about Timmy, and they were all so happy to hear that he recovered well.

Every single year, I went back to familiar faces, and made new friends, ones that wouldn't return, and some that soon would become friends that I'd be eager to see every year.

I got to the age where I would hand out with my friends more, and spent less time with Marjory and Tim. They allowed me to have some freedom, by going to the beach, or to restaurants with friends in the evenings, and we'd always

meet up at a certain place after dinner, and then all walk back to the apartments together. Ready to do it all over again the next day.

Claire, my sister, even joined us with her adopted mum a few times, which I absolutely loved. I have the most amazing memories of going there every year, and I would love to return one day.

Through the years

So, I have missed important things out in previous chapters. My siblings didn't just disappear from my life. We had regular visits, and days out as a big group, with our social workers.

We would all be dropped off at Harper Road Social Services, we'd spend some time there before we all left to spend the day together. Sometimes we would go around London, feeding the birds, seeing the queen's guards, a trip on the London Eye, eating at the Rainforest Cafe, and even had a visit to the London Dungeons.

But my all time favourite trip was to Freddie's Farm. Freddie had a huge farm, and kindly allowed us to help with the animals, collecting the eggs from the chickens, and we were even allowed to climb the very tall haystacks. I didn't go up too high though, it was a bit scary.

There came a time, when Freddie would no longer allow us to visit, I think he just wanted to get on with things, and not have a big group of children to entertain all day.

A few years after those farm trips stopped, I was watching TV, and there he was! Freddie, talking about his farm. It was strange to see him on TV, but also allowed me to remember the amazing times I had with my brothers, and sisters.

The visits with my siblings soon came to and end. It was difficult getting everyone together at the same time, so I didn't see them anymore, except Claire. Sometimes she would come to Marjory's house, and spend some time with me, we would have catch up, and tell each other what was happening in our lives, and then after a few hours, she would have to leave again.

The others, I didn't see for many years. I was okay with this though, I knew they were out there, and I knew that I would see them again one day. But for now, I had my life, and they had theirs.

Every time we met up as a group, it was always like we were never apart. It was always just so easy speaking to everyone, and seeing how they were all getting on. I even saw my previous foster carer once or twice, as at the point of these group visits, Aoife was fostering my younger brother. I wasn't overly fussed about seeing, or speaking to her though, it felt like she was almost a stranger to me.

She was just someone that I used to know.

I didn't care to talk to her, or to fill her in on how my life was going now. Marjory and Tim would talk, and have a quick catch up with all of the other foster, ad adoptive parents.

I found out at some point, that Marjory and Tim had short term fostered for many, many years before I arrived. They would in the future, go on to receive an award, and appear in the papers for their outstanding fostering work.

While I was with them, they had a little girl Lily, who stayed with us until she went off to her forever home. And then there was Billy, who went back home to his parents, and two older sisters. Helga came to stay with us for a week or two. Marjory had fostered her before, so Helga knew everyone in the house, except for me. We got on fairly well, she was nice to me, but boy, was she a bad egg!

Some children go through so many traumatic events in their lives, so they behave in the wrong way, and act out. But they may have grown up and witnessed their parents behaving in certain ways, and think that it's okay to also be this way. They've grown up not knowing anything different. And they can't quite process everything that has happened, they certainly don't want to talk about anything to anyone.

You'll often hear the familiar words of 'I hate you', 'You're not my mum/dad.'

But I promise you, we do not mean these things. We say these thing to hurt you in the moment, and may instantly regret the words that

spewed from our mouths. We just want you to hurt as much as we're hurting, so you can feel how we feel.

If I could give any foster carer, or adoptive parents any advice, I'd tell you to try and have patience. Be patient with the child you're caring for. Love them unconditionally, love them as if they are your own child. Do not treat them any differently, trust me, we see the difference, and it hurts. If you can be patient, and love the child, or children, you'll be okay. It's not easy looking after children anyway, but children who have had trauma in their lives, need a little bit extra of your patience, a little bit extra of your understanding, and a little bit extra of your love.

Marjory told us that another boy was coming to stay with us, he'd be severely disabled, but we would all do our best to look after him while he was with us.

I was so excited, and I couldn't wait for him to arrive. I don't remember the day that Ryan came to live with us. It sort of felt like he just, always there. He was a part of the family.

Ryan was such a special little boy, with many special needs. He had down syndrome,, severe delays, he couldn't talk, walk, sit, stand, or even move. So for everything he couldn't do, we loved him extra.

Ryan had a cot in the front room, oxygen tanks and wires filled the room, we played with sensory toys for him, letting him listen to the sounds that they made. Eventually we had night time carers come to the house, while Marjory and Tim slept, and got some well needed rest.

We would sometimes be allowed to sit, and hold Ryan, he was heavy, but I didn't mind, I just loved being able to be so close to him, I was in complete awe.

Ryan was tube fed, he only had his milk formula, and sometimes while holding him, I was also allowed to hold his tube up. My arm ached, a lot, but again, I didn't mind. Anything I could do for Ryan, I was always more than happy to do.

Ryan was often in and out of hospital, due to his many needs. The house always felt so empty without him, he made such a big impact on everyone's lives, so we really felt his absence whenever he was in hospital.

Ryan was born 16th September 2000, and at this point in my story, he was only three years of age, almost four.

Friday 9th July 2004 was really like any normal day. Ryan was in hospital, marjory was with him, Tim was at work, me and Shelly were at school. After school I went to girl guides, after a few hours, Tim picked me up, he was silent. We went to the car, and inside was shelly, she was crying. I asked her why she was so upset, and she snapped me, and told me Ryan had passed away.

This can't be true. She's lying. Surely she's lying.

My whole body went cold, I felt numb. I walked into the house, ran upstairs to my room, and fell back on to my closed door. The tears were pouring down my face, I was begging God to give him back to us. It wasn't fair that he was taken.

I wanted Ryan back.

Soon after getting home, we had to go and pick Marjory up from the hospital. Without Ryan.

Ryan wasn't coming home. I would never see his perfect little face again. I would never get to cuddle him again. My heart was broken. This was the first time I had experienced someone so close to me passing me away.

I HATED IT,

Things just weren't the same anymore without Ryan, everyone was sad, and everyone was always crying.

The day soon came for his funeral, everyone dressed up in their funeral clothes, and met at Marjory and Tim's house. Ryan arrived in the back of a hearse. How could his small body be in there? I still wanted him back. I couldn't process that he was gone forever.

We held Ryan's funeral at the local church, just up the hill, and around the corner. The ceremony had talking from the Vicar, everyone sung songs, and a few people got up, and spoke about Ryan.

The church was packed. Family, friends, nurses and doctors from the different hospitals Ryan went to. The church was filled with people sitting, and standing and the back of the church.

Ryan's family were among the people who attended. As a child, I hated that they even dared to come, and cry. They had no right to cry, and mourn for him. We were his family, we loved him, we cared for him, we did everything that they failed to do.

The time for Ryan to be carried out, and up until that point, I was doing well.

But seeing his small casket being taken out of the church, I lost it. I cried my eyes out. It was the hardest that I had ever cried. I felt like someone was ripping my heart out, and I could feel my heart breaking.

I walked down the church isle towards the exit, past all of the people, past Ryan's family, and I was sobbing uncontrollably. Marjory was next to me, holding me, cuddling me tight, telling me it would be okay. We all drove to the cemetery, and stood around, watching Ryan's casket being lowered into the ground. One by one, we each grabbed a fist full of soil, and threw it down. Some also threw flowers.

We then went to a nearby restaurant, to have the wake. Everyone sat down. They ate food, they had a few drinks, shared memories, and soon left.

We eventually had to go back home, back to the reality of never having Ryan home with us. We just had to learn to cope, and learn to slowly move

on without him.But we all still, to this day, hold him dearly in our hearts.

A special man

It had been a long time since I had seen my biological parents. I had mostly forgotten about them., I never even thought about them, they just didn't exist to me anymore. I now had a home, I had a family, I had parents who loved me. I had a really good life.

These biological parents meant absolutely nothing me.

I was ten year old when Marjory took me into the front room, and sat me down, to have a conversation with me. I knew she was going to tell me something, she looked sad, and quietly told me that Douglas had passed away, and that if I wanted to cry, or if I felt sad, it was okay to do so.

At that point of Marjory talking, I felt a hand touch mine, but nothing was there, I only saw my hands. I knew someone was there with me, holding me, making sure that I was okay.

But, I was okay. I was completely fine.

I felt nothing. I just did not care that he had died. Marjory was basically telling that a stranger has died. Was I supposed to care? I didn't.

He didn't deserve for me to feel anything for him. He certainly didn't deserve to even have a life anyway, after all of the despicable things he did to innocent children.

He deserved death.

Marjory spoke to our Vicar, and arranged for me to have a sit down with him, so he could talk about Douglas, and talk about him passing away, and see what my feelings were on the situation.

The Vicar spoke. I listened. But again, I just didn't care for the words being spoken. I didn't owe Douglas any of my feelings, or my tears, any of my love, or my time even thinking bout him. I went along with it because Marjory went through the effort to set it up, to help me, which I appreciated. But I also didn't need, or want.

When we arrived home, Marjory took me in to the front garden, and told me we could dedicate a little rose flower him, so I could remember, and think about him whenever I saw the roses. Again I went along with it for Marjory, I loved that she was trying to help. But I didn't ever want to remember him, or think about him. There were absolutely no happy memories to think about.

My memories are of sexual abuse. My memories are of a violent, disgusting drunk, who only cared for himself, and his own vile needs. They are not the memories I cared to reminisce about. To me, Douglas wasn't my dad. He was a man I unfortunately used to live with. The man that social Services failed to get me, and siblings away from for many years.

He did not deserve to be called a dad. He didn't ever do anything that a dad is supposed to do.

Tim is my dad. He was there for me every single day, he loved me, and cared for me how a dad was supposed to care for their child. I have so much love, and respect for Tim, and I always will. I was really close to him as a child, I was the typical 'Daddy's girl'. I loved him, and always wanted to be around him.

We would often sit in the kitchen, at the breakfast bar, and watch TV together. It was a daily routine for us to watch to watch the soaps, one after the other. And I loved every minute of it.

Tim was always so kind, and thoughtful. And although I never actually called him 'Dad', I always felt like he was. I often really, really wished that he was my real dad. I spent days wishing, and hoping that one day we would get a call from the hospital, telling us there had been a horrible mix up, and I was actually there daughter. That day, of course, never came.

Every time Tim went food shopping, I would always want to go with him, just to spend time with him. It didn't matter where we went, or how long for, I just enjoyed every second.

Tim would often go to Netto's and get me these own brand pies that they used to sell, as he knew I loved them, and knew exactly how I liked to eat them.

He would take the pie out of the packaging, cook it in the microwave, and then peel off the top, put butter inside, mix it up, squirt some ketchup in it, and finally put the top back on.

PIE PERFECTION.

I loved that he would do this for me, and would always buy the pies specifically for me. No one else was allowed them.

I know now just how much Tim loved me, and I appreciate it a whole lot more.

Tim is such a special man, the kind of man who deserves every happiness, and to get everything he wishes for in life.

Independence

I was 17 years old, and in college, seeing my friends every day, living a fun life, going to parties, spending my days and weekends at the local skate park, or at local gigs where the local rock bands played.

This was my life until my sister, Claire, asked me to move in with her. I jumped at the chance. I didn't think back then how much me moving out would upset Marjory, and Tim. It hit them both hard, but at the same time, they both understood that I needed to do this. I needed to become independent, and be with my sister again.

Claire now lived up North, in Lincolnshire, and so did four of my brothers. I was so happy to finally be seeing them all, and to be around them. It had been so many years since I had even seen any of my brothers.

I was at the very end of my college course, with only one week to go until I graduated, I explained to my tutors that I was leaving, and although they were sad to see me go, they wished me well with my future, and told me that I had done enough work to grant me a pass on my course.

And with that news, my college days were over.

I had a lot of friends that I was leaving behind. I was sad to be leaving them, but also equally as happy to be starting my new journey.

They understood why I was leaving, but also begged me to stay. They all said once I left, the group just wasn't the same anymore. I was the glue that held them altogether. And once I had gone, the group was gone, and they all went their separate ways.

I moved out just before my 18th birthday.

Darryl, Marjory's brother, and Marjory, both drove me up to Lincolnshire. It was an emotional drive, part of me wanted so badly to stay, but another part of me knew I needed to see this through, and move on to the phase in my life. There were stressful moments on the drive up, not knowing which road to go down, or where to turn, caused a few arguments here and there, while we all thought we knew which way was the right way. We got there eventually, and all arguments were forgotten about.We arrived at my brothers house, as this is where myself and Claire were staying for now. I said my goodbye's to Marjory, and Darryl, and they then left, and drove back home.

 So there I was, in Dan's house with Claire. Dan is our older brother, who shared his house with his then wife, Cleo. We gave them some rent money, it wasn't a huge amount, but it was he least that we could do seeing as they let us both stay until our place was ready to move in to.

We weren't at dan's house for long, before Claire and I moved in to our flat. I was now independent. I had responsibilities, that I just wasn't used to.

I was in way over my head. No-one had taken the time to teach me about bills, I didn't have a clue what I was paying out for. I gave all of my money to Claire's adopted mum, and she paid everything for me, out of my money, and would give me spending money as and when I needed it. This arrangement worked well for around two years or so, until all of my money had run out. My money all came from compensation, due to what we had been through, all of got it. And Marjory had also been saving up money to give to me when I left. But it was now all gone. All six thousand of it.

I had spent the last two years messing around. I was out partying nearly every night. Some good came from this, with the fact that I made some friends. Jess, and Cheryl, were my two main friends, who I would then spend a lot of time with making memories, that I will hopefully never forget. I don't think I would have survived my time in Louth with these two being by my side.

One night I had planned to meet them in a club, I went over to Kai's bar first, to see my brother who was a barman, and had some drinks there first, before I was to make my way over to the club. I was standing outside of Kai's bar, with my brother's girlfriend, talking to her before I was going to leave. When a few boys she knew walked up and started to talk to her.

They seemed to be good friends, and knew each other well. They mentioned that were heading to the club that I was going to, so my brother's girlfriend asked them if they would walk with me, so she knew that I would be safe.

They agreed, and we went our separate ways once we had reached the club. I would soon see them again, out side the club during our time there. While I was with my friend outside, she was smoking, the boys also came out, and saw me standing there, so came over to talk to us. My friend went back inside to dance, so I was left talking to Arran. Things were going pretty well, and I knew I liked him, I liked him as soon as I saw him earlier on at Kai's bar. We were there for a while talking, joking, and laughing. It soon led to Arran leaning in for a kiss.

My stomach was in knots at how exciting this was.

Arran was tall, with short, dark hair, and his green eyes glistened whenever I looked in to them.

We spent the rest of the night in the club together, getting to know each other. And when the club closed, we went for a drive with Arran's friend, and they drove me home. Arran walked me to door, and kissed me goodbye.

This was the start of our short relationship.

A few months later, we broke up.

The relationship got to a point where neither of us felt like carrying it on, we were more just friends than anything else. So I was perfectly okay with us splitting up. We didn't see much of each other after, maybe once or twice here and there. We'd say our hello's, and goodbyes, have a quick catch up, then go our separate ways again.

I saw him less, and less as time went on.

Young
& broke

I was thinking that my money would last forever. I had made no plans in regards to even finding a job when I moved. But now I had some growing up to do.

I had to find a job.

I luckily found one pretty much straight away. On a night out, I asked a barman that I knew if he knew of any jobs going anywhere, he told me he'd come back in a minute and let me know. He came back to me after a few minutes, and offered me a job in the club we were in, as a barmaid. Obviously I accepted, I was in no position to turn a job don at this point.

This was a great start, I was to get £50 per night. Now that I think back to it, I was seriously underpaid for the hours that I did, but at the time, I didn't question it. I was just happy to be earning some money. I had a job, and that was good enough for me.

Claire was moving out. She had met someone not long after we moved in together, and they decided to move in with each other. This left me at a bit of a loss. What was I supposed to do now? I only had a poor-paying weekend job, and was living in a two bedroom flat, that I definitely couldn't afford on my own.

I had to find someone to move in with me, and quickly.

I was in panic mode. I was desperate. Luckily one of my brothers was also looking for somewhere to live, so he soon moved in with me. This was great, as we got on really well.

Unfortunately, after a few months of living together, my money just wasn't enough to pay for my half of the bills. I was in over my head. I felt like I had nowhere to turn, and I just didn't didn't know what to do. My bank was in an overdraft, and I had no spare money to get out of it. I also had to move out, as my brother decided to move in with his girlfriend.

A friend of mine told me knew of someone who was looking to rent out their spare room. £20 a week, I jumped at it. This would have helped me out so much.

By this time, I had lost my weekend job as a barmaid. Just my luck. The manager had closed up, and run off with a lot of money. Everyone who worked there was out of a job.

Claire suggested to me that I should go to the job centre, and sign on.

I genuinely didn't know that this was even an option.

I went. I gave all of my details, and I waited.

While I was waiting, I applied for jobs in the town, and went to interviews. No jobs came up for me..yet.

Weeks had passed, I eventually received a letter saying because the person I was renting a room off earned too much money, I was not entitled to any money from them. I didn't question it. I just accepted it, and applied for more jobs instead.

Dan told me he knew of a job that was available, and if I wanted it, he would contact the lady, and give her my details. Dan did offer the job to Claire first, thinking she may have been interested, but Claire was now pregnant, so couldn't take the job.

After getting my contact details, the lady called me, and told me about the job. I expressed my interest, and she agreed to give me the job. We made arrangements for me to start straight away.

I was now a cleaner, earning a nice amount of money each week. I could now afford to pay the £20 a week for my room, pay off my overdraft, and even have nights out with friends on the weekends. Life was looking up for me again.

I went out for lunch with Claire, to Kai's bar. After we ate, we stayed a bit longer, chilling out, and having a few drinks, just enjoying our day.

A guy we both knew, and were friends with walked in with his friend that Claire also knew, but I hadn't yet met. They both spoke to Claire, while I sat there in silence. I noticed the friend looking over to me, but he didn't say anything. They soon left, and later that evening Claire told me that she was going to set me up on a blind date with someone. Claire wouldn't give any details away, other than where to, and when.

The day soon came for my blind date. I got myself ready, and went over to Kai's bar.

I sat waiting nervously for him to turn up. Wondering if he would in fact, turn up, or not bother at all. I was there for around 5 minutes before he walked through the doors. I was right, my blind date was the friend we had seen when we went lunch.

We didn't have an amazing date. It was a few drinks at Kai's bar, then on to a pub for a few more drinks. Then he walked me home. He did ask me out on a second date, and I agreed, hoping this second date would be better than the first. Wayne picked me up from my house, and we walked to his, only a short walk through town. He had cooked me dinner, and even made the dessert himself. I loved that he went to so much effort, I didn't know yet how I felt about him, I wasn't sure if I even wanted it to be anything more.

I decided I wanted to take it slow, and not put any pressure on myself for it to be more than just dating. During this second date, I excused myself, and went upstairs to use the bathroom. A minute or two later, I made my way back down the steep stairs, I missed a step, and slid all the way down. I was so embarrassed, but I laughed it off. I was fine, just extremely embarrassed.

Wayne then walked me home. And from there, we continued to see each other. It was a pretty basic relationship, we didn't go on dates, we just spent time at his house, always watching TV, or driving his friends around to different places.

We weren't seeing each other for long. A few month, and we were done.

Wayne's friend was always complaining that I was around, and he never got to be with friend, just them two anymore. I think Wayne got fed up with the constant moaning, and thought it was best to just end it. And although I wasn't overly keen on Wayne, I cried. Why did I cry for him? I was so upset that another relationship didn't work out. What was wrong with me? I couldn't make a relationship last longer than a few months.

Most people were happy to hear that we ended, with a few people telling me that they didn't even like him, or that we just weren't suited.

I decided to focus on myself from there.

So I got stuck in to work, and blew off steam by spending every spare minute I had with friends, partying, and drinking.

Over time I met new people, made new friends, carried on working, and partying. Doing what I could do to pass the days. I thought at the time, I was living such an amazing life. But now that I am older, I realise it wasn't much of a good life at all. But, I also wouldn't change anything, as it's got me to where I am today.

I lost my job.

I was unwell again, and I guess they thought that I was unreliable with being off so much recently.

I was fine with this, I wasn't happy with the job anymore, and I was already searching for a new one.

This did however cause issues with me no longer being able to afford to pay my friend for the room I was renting. He was okay with it, and said he'd give me time to find another job. That took a bit of pressure off,

But I couldn't find a job anywhere. No-one was hiring. I decided to go to the local council, and explain my situation. They agreed to help me, and passed me onto a local charity who helped care leavers find a place to live, with food boxes if needed, jobs as well.

Whatever was needed, they were there with a smile on their faces.

By this point, I was so fed up with my life in Lincolnshire, I wanted to go back home. I decided now was a good time for a fresh start, there was nothing left for me in Lincolnshire anymore. I obviously had my sister, brothers, and friends, but I needed more. I needed a place to live. I needed a job. I needed money. This area could no longer give me these things.

I told the charity that I would like to move back to London, and so they helped me with registering for Social housing there.

The charity's job was done. I was moving.

Claire's adopted mum was visiting Claire, and agreed to drive me to London, to other sisters flat, where I would be staying until my new flat was ready to move in to.

I was so grateful for the help, and I couldn't wait to go back, and start over again.

This time, hopefully doing it with a bit more maturity

Back to where it began

Back to where it began. London. Peckham to be exact.

It wasn't quite home, but it wasn't too far away.

I was staying with my other sister, and her husband, while I was waiting to get my keys and move in to my flat.

I was receiving regular money from the Government to help me. But most of this went on helping my sister pay for food, or pay her electric and gas bills. I barely had any spare to buy anything for my flat.

I was starting over, with nothing but a suitcase that had my clothes in.

My sisters friend, who I also had as a friend on social media, was coming over often, we had started seeing each other, despite warning from family members, I decided to go for it, and give him a chance anyway.

Eric was ten years older than me. I was excited that an older man wanted to be with me. I saw a friendly, mature man with a job. What could possibly go wrong? I didn't understand why I was being told not to get in to a relationship with him.

I was still unable to move in to my flat, as it wasn't ready. My sister was becoming annoyed that I started to refuse to pay all of her bills with the money that was supposed to be going towards furniture for my flat. She told me I had to leave.

Eric said I could stay with him while I was waiting for my flat to be finished. He found me furniture I needed, and even put down laminate flooring himself, to help me out.

But while this was going on, something wasn't right with me. My stomach all of a sudden became bloated, and hard. My periods were nowhere to be seen.

I planned to visit Claire, and travelled up with her adopted mum for a few days. She saw my bloated stomach, and got me to take a pregnancy test.

Two lines. I'm pregnant.

Once I got back home, I went to the hospital, and they did an emergency scan. There, on the screen, was a baby.

I was eight months pregnant, with roughly two weeks to go until I was due.

How on Earth has this happened?

My periods the last eight months were normal. I had no signs at all that pointed to a pregnancy, until now.

I had no choice now but to seriously change my attitude, and grow up, quickly. I called Eric, and told him what I had found out, he was adamant that he wanted to stick around, and raise the baby with me, despite this all happening very quickly in our relationship.

We took the next two weeks getting everything prepared, buying all of the things a baby would need.

My due date came, and went. I was four days overdue, and relaxing on the bed, when I felt a little pop, and felt as though I was leaking. I ran to the toilet, and I phoned Claire.

"I think my waters have broke. What do I do?" I whispered down the phone, in a panic.

Claire advised me to call the maternity ward, and let them now what was happening. I did just that. And off we went to hospital, to get checked over. I was in labour, and admitted to the labour ward. Despite the pain being bearable, I decided that I wanted an epidural. Soon after, my son arrived.

Ryan Tim Peerson was born 14th April 2010, weighing a healthy 7 Lbs 2 oz. I was over the moon. My small miracle.

I named him Ryan after my foster brother who passed away, and Tim, after my foster dad. They both meant so much to me, so I thought they were perfect names for my son.

Even though I was completely fine, and Ryan was doing well, we weren't allowed to leave the hospital. The midwife told me that they were waiting on advice from social services. I was in shock. What? Why? How are they involved? I was so confused. After four days of being in hospital, I was being discharged, finally.

But I was only allowed to leave under the conditions of me moving back in with Marjory, and Tim.

Social Services were worried whether I would struggle as a mum, and struggle to parent my child. They were under the impression that because of the trauma I had gone through as a child, this would affect my parenting, and I may turn out like my parents.

Determined to prove them wrong, I moved back in, and I did everything a mum should. I made fresh bottles every day, and night. I fed, I burped, I changed, I bathed. I went for walks, and days out. I was being the best mum I could be.

Social services were often after updates, asking Marjory how I was coping. Of course, Marjory only had good, positive news for them every time they asked.

But still, they questioned me.

I had a meeting with a social worker, we went for a coffee, and had a long talk about their concerns.

"Do you remember everything that went on back then?"

"How can we be sure that it hasn't affected you in a negative way?"

"We can't be sure that you won't neglect your son."

"What if you've buried your trauma, and one day, you remember what you went through, and then has a massive impact on your parenting."

I did my very best to convince them that I was nothing like my biological parents. I was angry that they even suggested this, but also understood their concerns. I explained that I was extremely lucky to find a really good foster family. One who gave me an amazing upbringing. I had foster parents who loved me, and helped me so much over the years, they taught me what was right, and what was wrong. I wasn't stupid, I knew very well that what my parents did was wrong, and I would never in a million years put my child through the neglect that I had gone through. I wanted to give Ryan the best of everything.

The social worker already knew how well I was doing, given the fact that they were getting

regular updates.

Two weeks were spent at Marjory, and Tim's. Social Services were finally satisfied that I was doing a great job in raising Ryan. I was finally able to leave and move in to my flat. Tim drove me and Ryan to my flat, but he didn't want stay, I think he was emotional about me leaving once again. I gave him a hug, and thanked him for driving us.

This was it. Me, Ryan, and Eric, living together. A family. Things were amazing, Eric went off to work, I stayed home raising Ryan, and taking care of the flat. This went on for around a year. Eric was now in between jobs, a lot. I had noticed that he had become quite lazy. He wasn't really helping much around the house, or with Ryan. Eric would stay up all night on his computer, playing games, and then as Ryan and I woke up for the day, Eric went off to bed, and slept all day.

February 14th, Valentine's Day. Eric wasn't an overly romantic person, so we didn't celebrate the occasion. But I had taken a few tests that morning. Four tests later, I admitted to myself that I was pregnant.

I took the tests to him. He was again, on his computer playing games. He didn't take much notice to what I was telling him. A nod, a slight grunt, and a brief "Cool," is all that I got from him. And this his game got his full attention again.

I was annoyed, but I left it. I didn't want to argue in front of Ryan.

A few weeks had passed, I was now around 8 weeks pregnant.

I couldn't get up. I was in so much pain. Eric got up with Ryan, although he barely did any parenting, as he spent most of the time on his computer as usual, leaving Ryan to entertain himself with toys. Eric only got up from the computer when it was time to feed Ryan throughout the day, or to change his nappy.

I however, was in the bedroom foe three days. Barely conscious, unable to move most of the time. I had to crawl to and from the bathroom when I needed to go. The pain that I was experiencing was unbearable, with the few seconds that I was awake, I begged Eric to call an ambulance. None of us knew the reason why I was in so much pain, it could have been serious.

Eric refused. Shouting at me, that they wouldn't come just for me having a bit of stomach pain. I was just left in the bedroom, alone, for three days.

The pain eventually stopped, I was able to get up again, and continue as normal.

My scan day arrived, so we all went to the local hospital. They were running late, and Ryan wasn't happy, so Eric took him home. I was left there to go through the ultrasound alone, which, at the time, I was fine with.

Ryan was better off going home so he could be happy with his toys, and have lunch.

I continued to wait, until it was finally my time to have the scan done.

On the bed I went. I lifted up my top, tucked tissues under my bra, and trousers, ready for the cold gel to be squeezed onto me. The sonographer got on with the scan, she was silent while moving the doppler around. She excused herself and said she was just getting the consultant to come and do the ultrasound instead.

The consultant came, and carried on where the sonographer had left off, rolling the doppler around all areas of my stomach. She turned the screen towards me so I could see. There was nothing on the screen. No baby was where a baby should have been.

"I'm so sorry, it looks like you've miscarried, we'll need to do a few more checks, to make sure you've fully miscarried, or if there's anything else that needs to be done."

I'm silent. Frozen. I had no thoughts going through my mind. Just complete silence.

I was asked to go in to the waiting room, while they get the report printed, that confirmed I had a miscarriage. They told me all I could do now was to go home home, and wait for the bleeding to start, and to keep an eye out for a blood clot, that would have been the baby.

I walked back home, and told Eric, he wrapped his arms around me, and said he was sorry. I didn't return his cuddle, or speak to him.

He made me some food, I ate it, although I wasn't hungry. I was just numb. I wanted to cry, but I couldn't. No tears came. I had to carry on as normal. I had to stay strong for Ryan.

Things with Eric didn't get any better. He would still spend most of his days sleeping, and nights playing computer games.

I went on his computer, and went to the history to find a website I had previously been on. But instead, I saw a lot of his previous searches. The same Facebook profile kept popping up, so I clicked on the links. Every single one was pictures of another female. I left it, for now.

His emails were also left open, as I went to sign out, I saw emails from a dating site, so I had a look. He had signed up, and had a profile. I went on to it.

Single. No children.

I questioned him about what I had found. He admitted to pleasuring himself to his female friend's pictures, and he admitted to being on a dating site. Why did I forgive him? I was so stupid.

I just let his behaviour slide, again, and again.

Eric had a friend, an old man, who he often did errands for. One day, Eric went to this mans house, to cook him dinner, and keep him company for a few hours. I was expecting him home, but the day turned into night, and he wasn't home. The day turned into two days, into a week, into a few weeks. Nothing. No Eric. No texts. No phone calls. My attempts to contact him were ignored.

I eventually decided that enough was enough. I got myself, and Ryan dressed, and we walked the twenty minute walk to where I knew he was, at this old man's house. Staying his spare room. Eric was angry that I had just turned up, without telling him, but he let me in, so we could talk. Turns out that Eric just wanted to play computer games, and do whatever he wanted. He agreed to come home, and change his ways.

He did, he sorted his sleep pattern out, and got a job. Everything was good again. A year had passed, and again, I was pregnant.

My pregnancy wasn't easy. I had horrible sickness, all day, every day, and night. The pregnancy went fairly quickly though, and before I knew it, my due had arrived. But Little Miss Stubborn was comfortable. She was a no-show. Eventually, I was admitted in to hospital to have an induction. Eric's sister took Ryan for us, so Eric could stay with me while I gave birth.

The midwife did the induction, and told me to get comfortable, as nothing would happen straight away. I asked to get an epidural, but I wasn't allowed one yet. I was told to wait. The pains came on very quickly, and within half an hour, I was in a lot of pain. I cried through it, but still, despite asking many times, the midwife told me to just wait.

"Go for a walk."

I couldn't walk through the pain.

"I'll run you a bath."

I sat down in the water, I barely lasted a minute before I had to get back out again. I dried myself, got dressed, and slowly made my way back to my bed I felt so sick at this point. I asked Eric to get me a sick bowl from the reception desk. So went to grab one for me, also telling the midwife that I felt sick, as he reached the desk. She came over to me and said, "Well, if you feel sick, I suppose I'll just do a quick checkup to see how you're progressing. I doubt much is happening though."

I took my trousers off, and spread my legs for her to check me over.

I was already fully dilated. And she could see the baby making an appearance. The midwife called for a wheelchair, and I was rushed off to the labour room. There was no time for an epidural now. I was doing this with zero pain meds. The midwives who were taking over, did their checks, and realised that my waters had not yet broken.

They covered themselves, fully expecting to have a big gush of waters explode onto them. But nothing like that happened.

I needed to push, so I did.

Effie Frances Peerson was born 13th September 2012, weighing 8 Lbs 9 oz, still in her sac. How amazing is that?

I was so exhausted from pushing, I didn't suggest to Eric to take any pictures, before the midwives took her out of the sac.

Eric cried, he was so happy. That was nice to see.

Reality

Soon after Effie was born, Eric went back to his old ways. He didn't bother going to work, he just wanted to spend all night on his computer, and all day sleeping.

A lot of arguments started, because of his behaviour,

I sometimes went on nights out with friends, to have a break, but every time I'd go out, Eric would accuse me of cheating. If I wore a top that was a little too low for his liking, I was called a whore. Eric started making comments about my body, telling me I was fat, I was letting myself go, I needed to lose weight. Despite only being a size 10 in clothes. I believed him. I soon hated my body, and the way I looked. I saw myself as actually being fat. I hated myself.

Even after speaking to me in disgusting ways, constantly accusing me of cheating, constantly shouting, and screaming at me, Eric still expected sex from me. And to keep him happy, I gave him what he wanted.

I decided to confide in a friend of mine, and I fully opened up, telling Sophie everything that had gone on. She told me that he was being a classic narcissist.

And the way he treated me wasn't right at all. She told me that I needed to end the relationship before it got even worse.

After our talk, I told Eric it was over. I couldn't carry on anymore. He had to move out. Eric was angry. He shouted, and screamed in my face about how I would never find anyone like him.

"Good luck finding anyone like me who will put up with you!"

"You're fat, and all you do is nag! You'll never find anyone else how will put up with your shit!"

And after that, he left. I was free.

I was now a single mum of two young children. But I was determined to carry on. I had to be strong for my children, and not let Eric's spiteful words get to me.

I enrolled Ryan into nursery, so he could socialise with other children his age, and this gave me time to spend keeping up with house chores, and seeing to Effie.

The years went by, with Eric picking and choosing when to be a parent, when to see the children, or when to pay towards things that they needed.

I always had to reassure Ryan, that Eric stilled loved him., And would see him soon.

Ryan was now at the age where he noticed Eric's long absences, and would always question it. I just had to try my best to reassure Ryan, and let him know that he would see his dad soon.

Ryan eventually graduated from nursery, and was starting primary school. Luckily there was a school across the road from where we lived, so the school runs were just a short walk.

Ryan had the loveliest teacher in his Reception class. This made the thought of leaving him all day much easier. I knew he as in good hands.

Eric met us at the school to see Ryan off on his first day. Ryan was so happy to see his dad. Eric spent a few minutes talking to Effie, who was standing beside me, then he left again.

I was in regular contact with Marjory. If I couldn't make the journey to visit her, and Tim, I would always call. Most days we were on the phone, having long conversations about our day. I would tell her everything that was going on with Eric, and everything to do with Ryan, and Effie. Marjory always gave me good advice, always encouraging me, and making sure sure that I knew I was doing a good job with raising them.

We didn't always see eye to eye, and would sometimes argue, and not talk for a while. But after we had cooled off, we would go back to our routine of daily phone calls, for catch ups again.

Tim wasn't ever much of a talker, so we rarely spoke on the phone. We made up for it when I visited them though, having conversations about how I was, what I'd been getting up to, spending our time together laughing and joking.

Through the years things pretty much stayed the same with Eric. He would sometimes see Ryan, and Effie, and there were times when he would be consistent, seeing them every weekend, and taking them on days out. I would invite him to stay over during the Christmas period, so he could wake up and see the children on Christmas day, and watch them open their presents. He, of course, slept on the sofa. I definitely wasn't ever going back there with him.

Then there were times when he would disappear for weeks at a time, with no message, or phone calls to even ask if the children were okay. I wouldn't get any financial help from him, because he was constantly in and out of work. Eric would either quit after a week, or two, or he would be fired. Because he couldn't stand to have someone telling him what to do. This would lead to him and many, many bosses having arguments, resulting in once again, being jobless.

I was doing really well in my life. The children were growing up, and doing well in school, I was slowly gaining my confidence back after Eric had taken it away from me, and I was getting back into part-time work, that fit around the children's school times. I was happy again. Finally things seemed to be working out for me.

Taking a chance on love

The year is now 2019, and everyone uses social media, frequently.

I would be on there daily. Either on my lunch breaks from work, or whenever I had a few minutes spare at home. There was a time when I received hundreds of friend requests, as did many other people on social media. I made my way through the list, deleting everyone I didn't know, accepting those I did, but as I was scrolling through, someone caught my eye. I accepted his friend request. We had mutual friends, so I thought I would give him a chance, and see what he's like.

We didn't talk much at first, a like of a status, or picture here and there. Until he posted a picture of a well known cartoon train, which I found rather amusing, so I commented.

We bonded over Thomas the Tank Engine.

We soon realised that we got on quite well, and had fairly similar interests, and personalities.

Greg added me to a few social media groups that he thought I would enjoy, as he enjoyed them as well. And he was right, I did. It was in these groups that we started talking more.

I posted a picture, one with a joke on, at the ned of it, it said something along the lines of "Apply in the Dms." Basically meaning that if anyone wished to take part in what the picture said, they could send me a direct message to express their interest.

Greg did just that. From there, we spoke throughout the day when we could, and this happened every single day. We would text from the moment we woke, every spare minute we had, until we would eventually go to sleep.

We grew really close, and both told each other that we had feelings for one another. After a few months of talking, we decided to make plans to go on a date. Eric was having Ryan, and Effie for the night, so I made I made my over to the hotel, as I had booked a room for the night, saved me having to travel back home in the evening.

Greg drove just over an hour to meet me. I was waiting in the hotel room, sat nervously waiting for him to arrive. When he did eventually arrive, I didn't talk. I was so nervous, he did talk either, he was also nervous. This was a great start. If we couldn't talk, how was this date supposed to happen?

Someone needed to break the ice.

Greg finally spoke. Phew. Ice broken. I was still nervous, and my stomach was in knots, my palms were all sweaty, and I felt physically sick from the feeling.

Greg took my hand, and locked his fingers in between mine, as we walked down the road to where there was a lovely little Italian restaurant. Sat opposite each other, we spoke, we ate, and spoke some more. I thought the date went really well, despite having a frosty start.

From there, we had many more dates. Every single one, we went to the Italian restaurant from our a first date. As time went on, and things between Greg, and I were going well, I decided he should meet Ryan, and Effie.

They were so excited to be meet Greg, but their excitement soon turned in to nerves as Greg pulled up in his car. We all walked over to a big park near where I lived, so the children could play, while greg, and I would sit and watch from the bench. Greg played some football with Ryan, and pushed Effie on the zip line, everyone had a good day. When we arrived back to my house, Greg revealed to the children that he had bought them sweets, their faces lit up at the big packet of Maoams that was placed in front them. They both thanked hm, and gobbled up their sweets.

They all got on so well. Both Ryan, and Effie, loved Greg already, which I was so happy about.

It's obviously so important when you have children, that when you're in a new relationship, they all get on well, so the relationship can continue to grow.

I also had to be careful, I didn't want to get in to another relationship for it to become like the relationship I had with Eric. I couldn't go through that again. I certainly couldn't put Ryan, and Effie through that.

I knew my worth. I knew what I deserved, and I knew that my children deserved a happy, non-toxic life. They needed to see someone love their mum, in the correct way. The way that any person should be loved. Not to see someone constantly shout, and tear their mum down every chance they got.

It seemed, with Greg, things were looking very positive. We got to see each other every other weekend, because Greg's job required him to work on some weekends. This worked for us though, we were happy with how everything was going between us. We continued to spends our days texting, laughing, and joking. I was so happy.

I fell in love.

Greg was the first person I had ever had such strong feelings for. This was true happiness.

I was never in love with Eric. I was young when we met, I was naïve. I thought that our relationship was normal. I thought that everything I went through with him, was what every relationship was like.

Greg was different.

I was comfortable with Greg. I could be myself with him, and I wasn't judged. He was always so nice, and respectful. I wasn't used to this. I wasn't used to being completely happy in all areas of my life.

Greg changed my life irrevocably.

Changes

Greg and I had only only been dating a few months before I found out that I was pregnant.

I was on the pill, that I took every evening, I didn't miss any. I wasn't ready for another child, nor was Greg.

My periods were regular. Every month, the exact day that I had worked out, I was on, without fail. So when I hadn't yet come on by 11ish that day, I was concerned. I knew something was up. I took a test, and then another, and another. Fourteen tests later, I sent Greg a message. He was at work, but I felt that he needed to know, I didn't want to wait until we would see each other again, as that could have been weeks away, due to him working most weekends.

After telling Greg, and getting over the initial shock, we both came to accept that I was in fact, pregnant. Fourteen tests couldn't be wrong.

Greg panicked. He wasn't ready for this. He didn't know what to say, or do. I had to reassure him that everything would be okay. I agreed that I wasn't ready for it either, especially as the relationship was still fairly new.

We had many, many conversations about. I quickly grew used to the idea. Greg, would take a lot longer.

I told a few people that I was pregnant again, including Marjory, Rachel, Sophie, and Claire. I also had to tell the mums ay school, as I was a part of Ryan, and Effie's school P.T.A, and we had a few events coming up, where I would be expected to lift heavy items when helping out.

Otherwise, I kept it quiet from everyone else.

I planned to announce it on New Year's day, but that didn't quite go to plan.

My scan day arrived. Ryan, and Effie were in school, I planned to take pictures for them to see. They wouldn't have been allowed to come anyway, as this was during the Covid outbreak. Greg had the day off work, so he came with me. When my name was called, I once again got on the bed, and sorted myself out, ready for the cold gel to be applied.

I was panicking on the inside, I was so scared that I would be shown an empty screen, where a baby should be, but isn't. I had nothing to worry about though, straight away we saw a small baby on the TV in front of us.

The sonographer did the usual checks checks, as we watched as they went through everything. After she had finished the scan, she explained to us that the baby had too much nuchal fluid behind the neck, which could be quite serious. She asked us to stay a little longer so a consultant could talk to us, and showed us into a small private room where we

could sit, and wait. The consultant came after a few minutes of us waiting, and asked us how we felt about what we had been told, and asked if it was okay to do another blood test, and have a CVS test done, so they could get some answers as to why there was too much nuchal fluid behind the baby's neck.

A CVS test is Chrionic Villus Sampling. This is a test that can be offered during a pregnancy, to check if the baby has a genetic, or chromosomal condition.

The consultant went through the procedure with us, and we both agreed that I would have it done, to get some answers. We were both led to another scanning room, where I was once again lying on a bed. But this time, I had a rather long needle pierced through my stomach, and into my placenta to collect some cells.

The pain was awful, and honestly, it was traumatising. I don't think I would ever agree to another one.

After the test he discussed everything with us, and told us the options of what we could do. Termination of the pregnancy being one of those options.

Absolutely not. No way. Not a chance.

They had no way of knowing then what chance this baby had, they didn't know what was wrong, or if anything was actually wrong, or how significant it was if there was something wrong. I turned that option down.

We had to wait two weeks for the results, and then we found out the baby had a chromosome deletion.

I had by then, already announced the pregnancy, and informed everyone of what was going on. As the pregnancy went on, I had many, many scans, of all types. And every time I went, I was asked if I wanted to terminate the pregnancy. It got to the point where I was so fed up with them asking me, I told them to stop, I couldn't take them asking any more.

At 33 weeks, the baby was measuring small, and the consultants briefly mentioned that I possibly would be induced a little bit earlier, depending on how the next scan went.

So, two weeks later, by myself, I returned for yet another scan. Greg wasn't allowed to come with me at this point, due to Covid restrictions, so he stayed at work, eagerly waiting for any news I had.

The baby hadn't grown in those two weeks, so it was decided that it was best for me to be induced sooner rather than later. I then made plans with the hospital to go in the next morning and be induced.

I made the rounds, phoning everyone, and giving them all the update, and of course, letting Greg know. Greg had to let his work know as soon as possible, and make plans to book the next few weeks off work. His work were luckily very understanding, and helpful with letting him off without much notice.

The next day arrived, and I made my way to the hospital. Greg had to wait in the car park until I was in active labour. He wasn't waiting for long. Inductions seem to work very fast for me, I was soon in active labour, and ready to be moved to the labour room. Greg joined, and a baby arrived.

17th June 2020, Grace was born, weighing a tiny 3 Lbs 11 oz.

Grace spent a few weeks in NICU, she had a few scary moments, with breathing apnea, needing oxygen, and many tests, but after three weeks, she was discharged from hospital.

With all of that going on, Greg was busy finding us a new, bigger house to move in to. Luckily, we were accepted for one close to where Greg worked, and the day that Grace came out of hospital, she had a home to go back to.

Ryan, and Effie, had spent those three weeks with their aunt, Eric's sister. So she drove the kids back to our new home, and had a quick meeting with Grace, before she had to get back to her children.

So there we were. A family of five. In our new home.

Ryan is now twelve years old, in secondary school, soon to be in year 8. Effie is nine years old, and home-educated. Grace has her chromosome deletion, wears glasses for an eye condition, and has delays in growth, and development. We have many different appointments for her, to give her the best chance in life.

Grace is a happy, and cheeky two year old.

Eric is still the same, absolutely nothing has changed with him, except his age. He picks when he wants to parent, decides when he wants to pay towards Ryan, and Effie, and still tries controlling me. I no longer give him that power, which is why many of of our arguments start. Because he doesn't like that he cant control me anymore,

Some days are hard, but every day is rewarding.

I have come so far in life. From the little girl who was neglected, and sexually abused, to the girl who wasn't wanted in different foster placements, finding a home with a foster family, who to this day, I still consider my family.

And now, living with the man whom I love so deeply, and three amazing children. And now, I'm an author. I turned a negative beginning, into a positive future.

I was lucky enough to be sent to foster parents who had the time, patience, and understanding to love me as if I was their own child. Not many children in the foster care system get to have what I found with Marjory, and Tim.

Marjory, and Tim played such a huge part in my life, and helped me to become the person that I am today. I will forever be grateful for having them both in my life. They no longer foster children, they had over thirsty years, fostering hundreds of children, and helped so many of them. Giving them a better future.

Each Peerson sibling are happily living their lives, some with families of their own, and doing really well in their lives.

I haven't seen, or heard from Barbara, my biological mother, in many years. And I don't plan on ever reaching out to her. Most of my siblings feel exactly the same way. We all have our own lives now, are are quite happy with never seeing, or speaking to her.

Poem written by Astrid Peerson

Why did I win the race that led to me being
here?

Born to parents who did not know how to love.

Alcohol, and violence.

A childhood ruined.

Innocence taken away.

Where am I?

Placed in the care of a stranger.

Tossed away, no care given.

On to another stranger,

My bags are packed again.

Another one, are you my new mum?

My fifth mum.

Am I safe here?

I feel safe.

My needs are being met.

Clothes, food, a bed.

I am cared for.

I am loved.

I am an adult. I am a mother.

A mother who knows how to love.

No alcohol. No violence.

No innocence ruined.

No strangers. No new mums.

I am your safe place.

I am your mother.

I win.

Printed in Great Britain
by Amazon

17594780R00061